1. Reflections on the Law of Love

Reflections
on
the Law of Love

Reflections
on
the Law of Love

James A. Griffin
Bishop of Columbus

ALBA · HOUSE   NEW · YORK

SOCIETY OF ST. PAUL, 2187 VICTORY BLVD., STATEN ISLAND, NEW YORK 10314

Library of Congress Cataloging-in-Publication Data

Griffin, James A.
    Reflections on the law of love / James A. Griffin.
       p.   cm.
    ISBN 0-8189-0608-1 (pbk.)
    1. Love — Religious aspects — Christianity.   2. Beatitudes-
-Criticism, interpretation, etc.   3. Corporal works of mercy.
    4. Spiritual works of mercy.   5. Christian ethics — Catholic authors.
  I. Title.
    BV4639.G75   1991
    241.5 — dc20   91-11889
                                          CIP

Designed, printed and bound in the United States of
America by the Fathers and Brothers of the
Society of St. Paul, 2187 Victory Boulevard,
Staten Island, New York 10314, as part of their
communications apostolate.

Printing Information:

Current Printing - first digit 1 2 3 4 5 6 7 8 9 10 11 12

Year of Current Printing - first year shown

1991	1992	1993	1994	1995	1996	1997	1998

Table of Contents

Preface vii

Part I: Beatitudes

Introduction 3
Happy are the poor in spirit 7
Happy are the sorrowful 11
Happy are the lowly 15
Happy are they who hunger and
    thirst for holiness 18
Happy are the merciful 22
Happy are the single-hearted 25
Happy are the peacemakers 28
Happy are those persecuted for
    holiness' sake 32

Part II: Corporal Works of Mercy

Introduction 37
To feed the hungry 41

To give drink to the thirsty 44
To clothe the naked 48
To shelter the homeless 51
To visit the sick 55
To bury the dead 58
To visit the imprisoned 61

Part III: Spiritual Works of Mercy

To admonish the sinner 67
To instruct the ignorant 70
To counsel the doubtful 73
To comfort the sorrowful 76
To bear wrongs patiently 79
To forgive all injuries 82
To pray for the living and the dead 85

Conclusion 89

Preface

In the post-Vatican II Church, the emphasis is certainly on the primacy of love. And that is good! After all, Jesus Himself summarized the whole of the law in the great commandment of love.

But "love" is a word with a great variety of meanings in our culture; it is a word which encompasses a wide spectrum of activities. So general is its breadth that "love" often becomes expressive of only vague and ill-defined realities. It seems to me that our Christian emphasis on the primacy of love must include a sharpening of the concept and a practical enumeration of the realities encompassed by this great law of love.

These reflections are an attempt to move in that direction. Using the Beatitudes and the Spiritual and Corporal Works as a starting point, I have tried to clarify what we mean by the "law of love," and to give concrete and practical examples of the Christian man or woman living according to this law of love.

I am grateful to those who helped me formulate these reflections by their suggestions, evaluations, and criticisms. Even more, I am grateful to those who have shown me the great law of love by living it out before my eyes.

James A. Griffin

PART I

Beatitudes

Introduction

We are sometimes accused of being a Church of "Thou shalt nots." I suppose that I would have to admit that this kind of view of our Church is possible, especially on the part of one who does not know the Church well, or deeply, or completely.

We are a Church with definite rules and a clearly defined code of conduct. We are the beneficiaries of the rules of life of the Old Testament, the Ten Commandments which are as applicable to life today as they were when they were given to Moses on the mountain. To these, we have added the rules of life which Jesus spelled out for us during His lifetime. Finally, we have the wisdom and the experience of the Church's nearly two millennia of history, as spelled out in her laws.

This is not a bad situation. We all like to have certainty in our lives, especially at the decisive moments of life. Some of us, by nature and temperament, long for even more than that. We long for clear-cut situations where everything is black or white; no gray areas allowed! Undoubtedly at times and in particular situations, we have as a Church, "oversold" this approach to a rule of life.

As I have mentioned, the Ten Commandments are still valid. They do serve as a general rule of life. They were the sealing of the Old Covenant between God and His people.

The Ten Commandments are cast in mostly negative terms. Jesus came and cast them in a new light.

When Jesus came, He announced Himself as not doing away with the Old Covenant, but rather as bringing it to perfection. He was to inaugurate a New Covenant between God and man, a covenant whose hallmark is love.

The sealing of that New Covenant is found in the Beatitudes. The Beatitudes are a positive description of the life of the follower of Jesus. The Beatitudes are found in the most important address of Jesus' life, the Sermon on the Mount. The great French writer, Bossuet, said: "If the Sermon on the Mount is the precis of all Christian doctrine, the eight beatitudes are the precis of the whole of the Sermon on the Mount."

We might view the Beatitudes, then, as taking us a step beyond the Ten Commandments. They carry us a step beyond the "thou shalt nots" into an area of "it is good for you if. . . ." They point out to us the road to happiness. In fact, the Beatitudes are sometimes called "the guidelines to happiness."

The Beatitudes are written in accord with a highly stylized form. Each Beatitude is composed of two parts: a principle and an interior result. The principle states the necessary condition for obtaining the interior result which is described.

Let me try to illustrate this for you by looking at Matthew's account of these guides, found in the fifth chapter of his gospel:

> "Happy are the poor in spirit;
>   the reign of God is theirs.
> Happy are the sorrowing;
>   they shall be consoled.
> Happy are the lowly;
>   they shall inherit the land.
> Happy are they who hunger and thirst
>   for holiness; they shall have their fill.
> Happy are the merciful;
>   mercy shall be theirs.
> Happy are the single-hearted;
>   they shall see God.
> Happy are the peacemakers; they shall be
>   called children of God.

Happy are they who are persecuted for holiness' sake; the reign of God is theirs." (Mt 5:3-10)

If you review this list as Matthew presents it, you will see that the principle is stated first. The interior result of adhering to the principle follows as a conclusion. It is noteworthy that the conclusions do not follow immediately. In fact, only two of these results are experienced in this life. The participation in the "reign of God" described in the first and last of the Beatitudes of necessity begins now. The other results are realized in the life to come. Let's take a detailed look at each of these Beatitudes. Let's reflect on these guidelines to happiness. It will not be a waste of time. After all, everyone of us is pursuing happiness. These are the markers of the road to true happiness. If we can deepen our understanding of them, we can hope to come to a deeper possession of happiness.

Father, love is the reason why You created us. Love is the end for which You created us. Help us to see Your love reflected in the law of the Old Testament and in the law of the New Covenant. May we, in turn, reflect that love in our actions towards others. Amen.

Happy are the poor in spirit,
for theirs is the kingdom of heaven

Notice again how the Beatitude consists of a statement of principle or way of acting, followed by the interior result. In this case, the ultimate result is the possession of Heaven.

In our reflection on this particular Beatitude, we have to be very careful to avoid either of two extremes.

On the one hand, we cannot so spiritualize our reflection that we, in effect, spiritualize the principle out of existence. On the other hand, we cannot water the principle down to a merely "this world" concern for the poor. We cannot equate "rich" and "poor" as they are seen from God's point of view with their merely material equivalents.

What does it mean, then, to be poor in spirit?

I believe that to be poor in spirit involves these elements:

First, we must depend on our God. We must look to Him as our rock, our anchor, our fortress. First and foremost, our trust must be placed in God.

Trusting primarily in our God necessarily involves detachment from things. This doesn't mean material poverty. A person can possess little or nothing and yet not be detached. On the other hand, one can have an abundance of this world's goods and be detached. Being detached means being ready and willing to walk away from all the things which "I possess," if necessary, to remain attached to God. What is at stake here is not just the quantity and the quality of the material things which I own, but rather the attitude which I have towards these material possessions.

To trust in God and to be detached from the things of this world demand that we be people of prayer. To trust and to be detached demand that we place God first in our lives.

If we are really going to be poor in spirit, God has to be "number one" in our lives.

The logic of this position is obvious. If anyone or anything else is number one in my life, then God cannot be number one. There cannot be two number ones! Closer examination will no doubt reveal that I am not detached from whatever surrogate number one I have in my life; in some way, my trust lies in this surrogate, and not in God.

The interior result of being poor in spirit is, as noted above, the possession of the reign of God. Again, the logic of this conclusion is obvious. If I am a person of prayer, if I have put God first in my life, if I have detached myself from all other things, then there is room and opportunity for God to pour Himself into my life.

And pour He does! Once we open ourselves to His gifts, once we make room for Him in our lives, our loving Father moves right in. We possess the presence of God; we possess the reign of God.

One author puts it in this fashion. He says that possessing the reign of God is not something which we could ever exhaust by any definition, but rather indicates a state of life in which our lives are centered on God and structured by His own mode of activity.

Here we reach the ultimate depth of meaning of this beatitude of poverty of spirit. God is most Himself in pouring Himself out in love. Those who are truly poor in spirit, who depend on God, trust in God, put God first in their lives, no longer seek to possess, but rather are possessed by the loving presence of God Himself.

Father, in the midst of all the things which I possess, help me to remain poor in spirit by keeping my life always open to You, by putting my trust totally in You, and by holding You always as the most precious element in my life. I look forward to being united with You in the richness of heaven. Amen.

Happy are the sorrowful, for they shall be consoled

This Beatitude seems to read like an open contradiction; the sorrowful are to be consoled. This seeming contradiction points up the paradoxical aspect of the style in which the Beatitudes were composed.

The seeming contradiction is explained by the difference between delayed gratification and immediate gratification. Remember what we said earlier. Except for the first and the last of the Beatitudes, the result which is promised is not realized in this life, but rather in the life to come.

This Beatitude leaves unexplained the deep mystery of human suffering. While no one can explain away this mystery, let me offer a few reflections on suffering which might make it a bit more understandable and therefore a bit more acceptable.

I once read a book which began with the line "Life is difficult." The author then went on to explain that, once a person realizes and accepts this stark and bold statement of reality, life becomes less difficult for us precisely because we expect difficulty in life.

The same is true of suffering. Suffering is difficult; but suffering does have value.

First, suffering tempers us. Suffering reminds us, at one and the same time, of our tenuous hold on life and of the necessity of our keeping our vision focused on what is really important in our existence. As tempering strengthens steel, so each bout of suffering strengthens us by adding some new quality of strength to our character. Equally important, suffering reminds us of our dependence on one another.

Second, suffering evokes sympathy from us. Here, I speak of sympathy in the truest sense of the word. It is only when we have suffered, it is only because we have suffered, that we can be empathetic to the sufferings of others. And, as experience teaches us, we can be most in touch with the sufferings of those men and women who are enduring the same sufferings which we ourselves are enduring or have endured.

Third, suffering brings our lives into conformity with the example of Christ the Savior,

Who came among us to show us how to live, and Who led a life filled with suffering.

The message of the example of Christ is that suffering, properly borne, draws us closer to God. We see this often in life. How it works, none of us can adequately explain, but that it works is obvious. We see it in the lives of others; we see it in our own lives. Suffering is redemptive. Suffering gives us insight and knowledge and wisdom which we are incapable of reaching in any other manner.

Apropos of our subject — the Beatitudes — we might point out that the same truth holds. It is more important that we believe that the Beatitudes work than that we understand how the Beatitudes work.

At its root, suffering remains a mystery. Although we can shed some light on the subject, we cannot penetrate the essence of this mystery. The problem of suffering is one of those ultimate mysteries of life which we can never fully grasp.

This second Beatitude reminds us that suffering, accepted in the name of God, leads to consolation. There is hope, even in the midst of our sufferings, as God Himself has promised us, that those who bear the sufferings of life in His name will experience consolation themselves. Suffering cannot be avoided in life; suffering, accepted with the right attitude, is truly redemptive!

Father, I pray that when suffering enters my life, as it enters the life of every person, I will be able to see the redemptive value of that suffering. May it draw me closer to You! Even in the midst of suffering, may I remain confident of the consolation offered to those who suffer in Your name. Amen.

Happy are the lowly;
they shall inherit the earth

To understand this Beatitude, we have to first correctly understand the term "lowly." The lowly are the "anawim" of the biblical community. These are the people who possess nothing, who are not gifted in any obvious way. The lowly are the people who are not pursuing power, those who are not trying to amass influence, not seeking to always be in a position to "pull strings" to obtain their own goals in life. We might understand these lowly well if we pictured them as being those upon whom the world looked down. The world despises or ignores these people because they do not live up to the expectations of the world. These people do not do what the rest of the world expects them to do. They treat the gift of life differently; they march to the beat of another drummer.

Again, we might more clearly grasp who the "lowly" are if we pictured them as men and women who treat the gift of life gently.

The majority of us are anything but gentle in the way in which we treat life. We are engaged in an ongoing wrestling match with life. We are anything but gentle in the way in which we treat this precious gift. We continually push and shove at life. We use all of our little tricks to manipulate life to get it in just the position in which we think we want it to be.

Both paradox and mystery are present in this Beatitude. The paradox is that those who are lowly, who are gentle with life are going to be the people who inherit the land. The mystery contained in the statement of this Beatitude is the mystery of Divine Providence. It is the mystery of the loving, gentle way in which God our Father takes care of us, His children.

For me, the lesson of this Beatitude is that it is those who are gentle with life who will inherit the land because God will deal gently with those who deal gently with His precious gift of life.

As if to guarantee the future promise which is contained in this Beatitude, God has give us the example of His Son. Although higher in dignity than the angels, Jesus humbled Himself, accepted the form of a man, and fashioned for us "the" example of being lowly. He dealt gently with all of life, even with those who persecuted Him and hung Him on the wood of the cross. And He inherited everything! As St. Paul says, "God gave him a name which is above every name so that at the sound of the name of Jesus, every knee must bend on the earth and under the earth, and every tongue proclaim that Jesus Christ is Lord" (Ph 2:10-11).

This gentleness was not limited to His own life alone. In the lives of those whom He drew close to Himself, in those with whom He associated, those whom He cured, Jesus showed a special preference for the gentle. It is as if by His actions He were saying to us: "Look here! Here is a lowly one. Learn from him; learn from her."

He put this in His own mouth when He said: "Learn from me, for I am gentle and lowly of heart" (Mt 11:29).

Father, help me to accept life as it comes from your hands. Allow me to be gentle with every circumstance of life and with every person who enters my life. In every situation, enable me to "let go and let God."

Happy are they who hunger for holiness;
they shall have their fill

At times, we have all experienced the pangs of hunger or thirst. We know how strong these pains can be. When we are confronted by them, it is hard to think about anything else than assuaging these longings. All we can concentrate on is that we really want something to eat or drink; and we want it now!

This is the type of desire which is depicted in the statement of the principle of this Beatitude. The Beatitude tries to describe that person who really longs for the fulfillment of God's will in this world.

There is a paradox here. In the very act of thirsting and hungering for holiness, we assure ourselves of having it.

We can begin to understand the paradox better, and understand this Beatitude better, when we grasp the difference between "possessing" God and being in deep personal "union" with God.

We cannot possess God. No one possesses God. Yet, often when we are beginners in the spiritual life, we talk and act as if that were indeed our goal. We see holiness in a simplistic but self-centered way; we see it as our possessing God to the fullness of our being.

The reality of the situation is quite the other way around. Instead of us being filled with God, we are called to collapse self into the reality of God, thus obtaining a deep personal union with Him.

This "collapsing" of self into the reality of God is no easy trick. It demands recollection; it requires quiet time for reflection.

We spoke earlier of the Beatitudes as being attitudes which the Christian should have when facing life. This Beatitude is a good example of that characterization; it brings out clearly that aspect of Jesus' positive description of the Christian life. This Beatitude describes a "posture towards reality" or a disposition towards life which ought to mark every action of our existence.

To have a posture or a disposition which is characteristic of all of life does demand recollection and reflection. "Put a little quiet into your life" is the watchword of this Beatitude.

Such an approach to life is certainly counter-cultural. Ours is a society filled with noise. We live with noise in our streets, our factories, our offices, our businesses. Then, we invite noise into our homes. How often, the first thing which we do when arriving home is to flip on the television or the stereo. It is almost as if we cannot bear to be without noise in our lives.

One winter vacation, I went to Florida to relax in the sun. I was amazed at the number of people who could not even enjoy the beauty of a walk along the beach without being "wired" with their radio headsets.

There is a popular telephone commercial which encourages us to "reach out and touch someone." This Beatitude sounds the opposite message. It calls us to quiet, to reflection, to recollection; by means of these activities we can "reach out and touch God."

The interior result which is promised by this Beatitude is fullness. It is not that we will have no desires, but rather that our every desire will be fulfilled.

The unknown author of *The Cloud of Unknowing*, one of the great classics of the spiritual life, summed up this lesson well:

> "The ideal is not for us to control our appetites at all, but to allow them full reign in the wake of an uncontrolled appetite for God."

Father, help me to realize that You speak to me in the quiet moments of life. Assist me in building quiet into my everyday life. Help me to grow in a deep personal union with You. Amen.

Happy are the merciful;
Mercy shall be theirs

I view this Beatitude on mercy as a distilla-
tion of Jesus' words and actions in relationship
to this subject.

The Scriptures are filled with examples of
Jesus' own merciful outlook. Consider His parables of the prodigal son and of the lost sheep.
Look at His treatment of the woman caught in
adultery and of Peter's denial. Reflect on His
promise that "In the measure you give you shall
receive, and more besides" (Mk 4:24) and that
"he who loves little will be forgiven little" (Lk
7:47).

It is most interesting to note that there is no
case recorded in the Scriptures of Jesus deny-
ing mercy to anyone who sought mercy from
Him, or who even opened self to the possibility
of receiving mercy from Him. Clearly, by His
actions, Jesus was demonstrating that, while He

will come as the Just Judge at the end of the ages, He comes now as the Lord of Mercy.

This is the age of mercy. As children of this age, then, we are called to be merciful in the likeness of the example of Jesus Himself. "If you forgive the faults of others, your Heavenly Father will forgive you yours. If you do not forgive others, neither will your Father forgive you" (Mt 6:14).

The mercy which Jesus proposes is a sharp contrast from the Lex Talion, "An eye for an eye, a tooth for a tooth." No, the mercy which Jesus offers is much different. It is a mercy which is given recklessly and disproportionately.

This mercy which Jesus speaks of is given without restraint to those who seem to be the least likely of possible subjects for mercy. More, it isn't given in any logical proportion to the merit of the subject. It is given to those who seem incapable of changing their own lives. It is even extended to those who seem to have little intention of reforming. "Forgive them, Father, for they know not what they do" (Lk 23:34).

Jesus extends mercy, in a word, even to those who do not seem to be forgivable. Why? He does so because He is the Lord of Mercy, and this is the age of mercy.

You and I are called to have a similar attitude. We are to extend mercy recklessly, even

23

to those whom we judge to be not worthy of our mercy. After all, if we judge them to be worthy of mercy, we would be moving into the virtue of justice and reflecting characteristics of the age of justice. But, that is not the case, as we are followers of the Lord of Mercy and we live in the age of mercy.

Mercy is a difficult attitude to integrate into one's life. But, the interior result promised is one of those ". . . and they lived happily ever after" endings.

The interior result of being merciful is the reception of mercy in return. When you are merciful, you are putting yourself "in union" with the mercy of God Himself. Being "in union" with the mercy of God assures you that this same mercy will be yours . . . forever.

Father, help me to become a child of "the age of mercy." True to my heritage, help me to offer forgiveness to others and, in return, to be the object of Your merciful and forgiving love. Amen.

*Happy are the single-hearted,
for they shall see God*

Consistency is a major thrust of the statement of the principle of this Beatitude. Being single-hearted on occasion is not difficult; being single-hearted consistently is no mean feat. We know, from many areas of our life, how difficult it is to be consistent. Hardly any of us succeeds in always being consistent because there are so many distractions in our attempts to be consistent. Yet, as we also know from a myriad of lessons gleaned from life, hardly anything worthwhile in life comes without persevering effort. In our relationships with others, we all realize how much easier it is to understand and to work with a person who is consistent in his or her judgments and decisions, even when those judgments and decisions do not parallel our own.

To the eye of the casual observer, significant discoveries often seem to come "in an instant." But a little research into the background of such discoveries usually reveals that those involved put in years of effort in their research. Then suddenly, the light came on and they could say, "Oh, now I see . . . it's so simple!" The instant of discovery usually rests on the foundation of years of consistent effort.

The same holds true in the spiritual life. The consistency of having one goal in life, of putting God number one in life, of giving Him the unswerving allegiance of our hearts, will result in the simplicity of vision which draws all of life into the simplicity of God Himself.

We can see this lesson beautifully exemplified in the life of St. John, the beloved disciple of the Lord. John authored the Book of the Apocalypse, the most difficult and involved of all the New Testament writings. The intricacies and the convolutions of John's reflections on faith and on salvation history contained in the Apocalypse defy explanation or understanding.

Yet, years of single-heartedly living the faith brought St. John to the simplicity of vision which is presented in the statement of this Beatitude. We are told that when St. John was a very old man, the members of the Church community would carry him to their Sunday assemblies on the island of Patmos. As he had been the "beloved" of the Lord and most likely the only member of the community who had actually seen Jesus, it was natural for the members of this worshiping group to turn to John and say, "Speak to us. Tell us of the Lord. Give us a message of faith, a watchword for life."

St. John's regular response was the verbalization of the interior result of this Beatitude. "Little children, love one another."

When I reflect on this Beatitude, my own episcopal motto comes to mind. That motto is: "Rooted in Christ." If we can succeed in rooting our lives in Christ, then He becomes the wellspring, the source of our life. Our hearts live because of His heart. We then truly become single-hearted. We see all things as God sees them, and what God sees is . . . Himself.

Father, grant me the gift of vision to see all of life in You. May every event of my life be anticipated, received, and accepted with a single-hearted love of You. And, may a lifetime of seeing all things in this manner bring me to the vision of Yourself.

Happy are the peacemakers;
they shall be called children of God

We all recognize that peace is an attitude. Peace consists of a right attitude or a right relationship with God, with neighbor, and with self. It is only when we have these three relationships in proper balance that we can speak of being "at peace."

The peacemaker is the person who pursues this right relationship.

Lack of peace is much in evidence in our society today; this triple relationship is often strained or broken. The peacemaker is called upon to respond to our society's lack of peace. The peacemaker responds by action, yes; but, even more, the peacemaker responds by attitude.

The peacemaker responds by action. The peacemaker seeks to maintain these right relationships and to lead others to the same posture in life. A peacemaker encourages others to accept self, to heal estrangements, to resolve conflicts, to turn back to God.

This is all part of being a peacemaker. But the heart of this Beatitude, as of all the other Beatitudes, is again found in an attitude or outlook on life.

What matters most for a peacemaker, then, is not so much success or lack of success, but rather to stand as a sign of peace to this world. To be a peacemaker is to proclaim the message of hope and redemption in the midst of an often hopeless and sin-filled world. The peacemaker stands as a sign of the reality of peace through his or her actions, and as a sign of the possibility of peace through his or her attitudes.

The interior result of this Beatitude presents an interesting contrast with that of the other seven. It is the only case in which the term "called" is used. Peacemakers are to be "called" the children of God.

In the use of this specific term "called," I believe we find a deep insight into the interior result of this Beatitude. To understand what I mean, go back to your own experiences in life.

You often call people "children" of their parents when you see the attitude of the parent reflected in the life of the child. Witness our saying "like father, like son" or "like mother, like daughter." Sometimes the behavior referenced is positive; at other times, the referenced behavior is negative.

Parents too are proud to call their offspring their own when they see their own best traits reflected in their child. They boast "that's my boy" or "that's my girl." They are quick to "call" them their children when they see the best of self reflected in them.

It is just so with the gift of peace. God is proud to call us His children when He sees His own gift of peace reflected in our actions and in our attitudes.

St. Francis of Assisi captured the heart of this Beatitude in his beautiful peace prayer:

> Lord, make me an instrument of Your peace.
> Where there is hatred, let me sow love
> Where there is injury, pardon
> Where there is doubt, faith
> Where there is despair, hope
> Where there is darkness, light.
> And where there is sadness, joy.
>
> O Divine Master, grant that I may not
> so much seek to be consoled as to console.
> To be understood as to understand.
> To be loved as to love.

For it is in giving that we receive
It is in pardoning that we are pardoned
And it is in dying that we are born
To eternal life.

Father, help me to reflect that right relationship with You, with others, and with myself which will mark me as being your child. May I be at peace! May I bring peace to every person and to every situation which I meet in life. May I truly become an instrument of Your peace.

Happy are those persecuted for holiness' sake; the reign of God is theirs

We begin our consideration of this final Beatitude by pointing out that, like the very first of the list, this Beatitude announces an interior result which is present now. It is not reserved for the future as with the other six Beatitudes. It is presented as a reality of the here and now.

We also begin our consideration of this final Beatitude by reminding ourselves that, as in the case of the other seven, we are dealing with a description of an attitude of Christian life, an enduring manner of thinking, feeling, and acting.

Who are those who suffer persecution for holiness' sake? Are they not those who are suffering in China, Lithuania, Central America, Northern Ireland, and other sections of the world because of their faith? Certainly! But does not "persecuted for holiness' sake" also include those who are excluded from certain social circles because of their faith? Does not this description encompass those who are shunned or made the butt of jokes in offices and work places because their faith does not allow them to accept the gross manner of speech so prevalent in our society? And does not the "persecuted for holiness' sake" include those, especially among our youth and young adults who, again because of their faith, cannot accept the standards — or lack of standards — of sexual morality which are presented as "the norm."

"Persecuted for holiness' sake" includes all who suffer because of their faith, provided that their suffering is accompanied by a correct attitude.

This correct attitude towards suffering has its birth in the realization that suffering is to be expected as a part of the life of each of us. Did not Jesus say, "Take up your cross and follow me" (Lk 9:23)? We are each called upon to accept the reality of the mystery of suffering in our lives.

This correct attitude towards suffering finds its growth in the realization of the truth proclaimed by St. Paul that, by our sufferings, we build up and supply what is lacking in the Body of Christ, His Church (cf. Col 1:24).

This correct attitude towards suffering finds its perfection in the acceptance of the mystery that we should rejoice in the knowledge that we have been chosen and found worthy to suffer in imitation of Jesus Himself. Then, this becomes a great attitude; it becomes gratitude!

"The reign of God is theirs." By accepting this attitude of trusting acceptance of the mystery of suffering, the Christian proclaims belief in the ultimate arrival of the Kingdom of God. More, the Christian proclaims conviction that this Kingdom is "in process of arrival and perfection at this moment."

Those who live out this Beatitude participate in the arrival of God's Kingdom by their acceptance of the suffering of "persecution for holiness' sake." Those who live out this Beatitude participate in the perfection of God's Kingdom by their stance or attitude towards suffering. In every sense of the word, then, the reign of God "is" theirs.

Father, when suffering comes into my life, let me not struggle with "why" or kick against the goad or rebel in other ways. Rather, give me the courage to accept suffering as part of the human condition. Through my endurance and acceptance of the gift of suffering, may I both build up Your Kingdom and build myself into Your Kingdom.

PART II

Corporal Works of Mercy

Introduction

When I was in school, it seemed we memorized many of the facts about our faith. I don't think this approach was at all bad. We knew the principal truths of our faith. If there is any legitimate criticism which can be leveled against this approach, it would be that at times we were not encouraged to completely understand what we memorized, or to put those words into action as part of our lifestyle. And this, in the final analysis, is the end of all religious study — to live out what we learn. Faith is "facts for living"! One of those sets of "facts for living" which I memorized as a boy, was the Works of Mercy. What a plan of life they set before us. Do you remember them?

You probably recall that these Works of Mercy are divided into two categories: Corporal and Spiritual.

The Corporal Works of Mercy (from the Latin word "corpus" or "body") are those actions which provide assistance to another's bodily needs. With that introduction, can you remember them?

> To feed the hungry
> To give drink to the thirsty
> To clothe the naked
> To shelter the homeless
> To visit the sick
> To bury the dead
> To visit the imprisoned

The Spiritual Works of Mercy address the internal or spiritual needs of other persons. Because they are more ethereal in nature, they are usually not as easily recalled as the Corporal Works of Mercy. How well could you do?

> To admonish the sinner
> To instruct the ignorant
> To counsel the doubtful
> To comfort the sorrowful
> To bear wrongs patiently
> To forgive all injuries
> To pray for the living and the dead

Let's review these Works of Mercy. At the end of our reflections, we might find it easy to recall these basic facts of faith. Even better, we may have managed to raise our own consciousness about opportunities to put these Works of Mercy into practice, weaving them into the tapestry of our lives.

We begin with the question: "Where do the Works of Mercy come from?" Indirectly they have their origin in the Scriptures. All of these activities are praised in various parts of the Bible. More directly, we can find these works reflected in the public life of Jesus Himself. Jesus teaches and lives these works in His public life. Most directly, these Works of Mercy, listed as we have them now, come from the living tradition of our Church. They can be traced back in their present formulation to the Fourth Century.

The origin of these Works, as well as the very nature of their contents, tells us that they do indeed form an ideal pattern of life for us to strive to follow.

As we reflect on these Works of Mercy, why not memorize them yourself? There are a lot of less worthwhile facts that we all commit to memory. And as those teachers who taught me knew so well, knowledge is indispensable to practice. Let's then, review these Works of Mercy together, seeking to integrate them more fully into our own Christian lives.

Father, may the works of my life be reflections of the great commandment of love. May each of these works reflect my abiding love for You and my willingness to extend myself in order to meet the needs of my sisters and brothers. May the memory of these works be the legacy which I leave this world.

To feed the hungry

We can easily link up this Corporal Work of Mercy with the ministry of Jesus. The most outstanding example of feeding the hungry was the occasion on which a crowd had been following Jesus for some time. It was late in the day, and the people were hungry. The Bible says that "Jesus had pity on the crowd . . ." so, He took a few loaves and fishes and miraculously multiplied them to feed the thousands (cf. Mt 15:33 ff).

Most of us, when we think of feeding the hungry, think of giving a poor person a handout, or preparing a food basket at Thanksgiving or Christmas. Certainly this is "feeding the hungry." But these activities just touch the surface of the problem. Thanks to the marvel of almost instantaneous communications, we see the hungry of the world up close and personal via television. In our own communities, there has been great emphasis in recent years on addressing the needs of our hungry on a more regular basis through soup kitchens, food pantries and other organized programs.

Ask yourself: Is there a way in which I can be responsive to the hungry on a more regular basis? Can I donate food to my parish or to another organization regularly? Or, can I contribute to a collection for the poor? Or better, can I give of my own time and talent at a food pantry or a soup kitchen?

Even in our complex society, there are still ample opportunities to feed the hungry in a more personal way. Perhaps there is an elderly person near you who is hungry because he or she is not eating good meals. It is difficult to prepare a balanced meal when one eats alone. More difficult, when one is elderly and alone. Or perhaps there is a large family you know which could use some supplement to its food supply. Some "extra" or "special" item that such a family ordinarily would be unable to buy.

I think that almost all of us are in a position to be able to share something with the hungry. The task is for us to be sensitive to the needs of the hungry, to remind ourselves that this problem of hunger exists around the world and even in our midst and to respond in some appropriate and positive manner.

To raise our consciousness doesn't demand any new activity or new time allotment. Every time we sit down to a meal, when we say our thanks to God before we eat, we can have that grace before meals be a reminder to us of those who are not going to sit down to a meal that particular day.

Perhaps this feeding of the hungry is listed first among the Works of Mercy because it addresses the most basic need of physical life — food. Or perhaps, it is listed first among the Works of Mercy because Jesus used this giving of food as a type or example of the spiritual nourishment of Himself which He gives us in the Eucharist. In any event, feeding the hungry is a fitting Corporal Work of Mercy for us to memorize and to incorporate into our daily life.

Father, may the moment of grace before each meal be just that for me, a moment of grace in which I realize anew how You pour Your gifts of love upon me, day in and day out. Let me never take for granted any meal, nor any moment of the unbelievable gift of life which You give to me.

To give drink to the thirsty

I indicated at the beginning of our consideration of the Works of Mercy that all of them are reflected in the life of Jesus. This particular work of giving drink to the thirsty, we might say, marks the beginning and the end of Jesus' public life.

At the very beginning of His public life, at the wedding feast of Cana, Jesus anticipates the thirst of the guests at the wedding by turning water into wine. And at the end of His public life, as He hung upon the cross, among the very last words of Jesus is an expression of His own need of a drink: "I thirst."

Perhaps there is a special lesson for us in the fact that Jesus' request for a drink was not answered, but it was responded to in such a mocking fashion. Could it be that His unanswered request for a drink stands as a special challenge to us, His followers, vis-a-vis the needs of our brothers and sisters?

A drink of water seems like an insignificant item. Most of the time we hardly advert to it. But there are times when a glass of water is golden — if we're sick, or if we have been working hard or exercising strenuously on a hot day, or if we've been out in the desert (I recall a trip into the Sahara Desert where water was severely rationed for two days). On occasions like these, nothing matches a glass of cold water, not even a Bud Light!

But perhaps another application of this Work of Mercy is possible. Could it be that Jesus' indication that not even a glass of cold water given in His name will go without its reward (Mk 9:40), contains an even deeper significance? Normally a drink of water is among the most insignificant of another's corporeal needs. Is not Jesus indicating here that attending to even the most insignificant of the physical needs of our brothers and sisters will not go unnoticed or unrewarded?

Now for some practical applications, some ways to integrate this Work of Mercy into our everyday lives: Consider Jesus' anticipation of the thirst of others at the wedding in Cana. Isn't it possible for us at times to anticipate the thirst of others, to offer them a drink of water or a cup of coffee when they visit, or in the midst of a busy work day, or at the end of the day when they gather at home?

How many other opportunities do we have to anticipate the needs of others for a drink — the mailman who comes to our door on a regular basis in extremes of cold and heat, the neighbor or family member who cuts our grass or rakes our leaves or shovels our snow, the friend or acquaintance who has just received bad news and needs our companionship over a cup of coffee? All of us, if we examine our own daily pattern, can find ample opportunities to value the gift of water in a new light and to share it with a new meaning.

Or in these days of concern and attention to our environment, shouldn't this work of mercy serve as a reminder to us to value the gift of water? How much of this world is without running water? How many people have to devote the major part of their day just to hauling in a sufficient supply of water? Yet we take water for granted, and we waste it with abandonment as we wash, shave, shower, cook. Jesus' example in His words about water should serve as a reminder to all of us of the precious — and limited — gift we possess in fresh water.

Father, make me always sensitive and attentive to the needs of others, starting with those to whom I give the special name of "family" or "friend." Allow me to realize how gifted I am, and how I can use these gifts to respond to the needs of others, in imitation of You, and in Your name.

To clothe the naked

This is a Corporal Work of Mercy which is reflected in Jesus' life only in a negative way. One of the sufferings which Jesus endured at the end of His life was being naked upon the cross. We can all empathize with the embarrassment and the humiliation which He suffered. How humbled we are if we have to don a hospital gown, or even if we have to appear in a situation in which we do not feel "properly" dressed.

Besides being a response to our very nature, clothing the body is a Christian sign of our respect for the body as a temple and place of indwelling of the Holy Spirit. A significant aspect of this Christian respect for the body is reflected in adorning it with proper and fitting clothes.

I indicated earlier that this Corporal Work

of Mercy is reflected in the life of Jesus in only a negative manner. It is most likely reflected in the lives of most of us, also only in a negative way, as most of us have "too much" clothing.

This is a Work of Mercy which is easy for most of us to practice if we just advert to it and take the time. Take the time — that's the key here. If we only take the time to go through our clothes, most of us will not only find useful clothing that we don't use, we'll find clothing that we know that we will never use! Sorting out these items gives us an easy opportunity to practice this Corporal Work of Mercy of clothing the naked.

There are many reminders of the needs of others for clothing. Most parishes have St. Vincent de Paul members who collect these items. Our shopping centers are dotted with drop-off boxes of various organizations who collect clothing for those in need. Some parishes have special collections or special days in which useful clothing is collected, separated and sent on to the needy.

Again, this is a Corporal Work of Mercy which provides ample opportunity for a "one to one practice." Sharing clothing with members of our own family, handing down items from child to child, giving items to relatives and friends when we no longer use them, are all fulfillments of this Work of Mercy.

I suggest that indirectly we address this Corporal Work of Mercy by the way we dress our own body. Dressing in a manner fitting our Christian vocation, even when it runs contrary to the customs of our society, is an indirect recognition of the message of this Work of Mercy. Coming to Church dressed in our Sunday best, is both a recognition of the value of one's own body, as well as a recognition of one's status before God.

There is a saying which we often hear in reference to dress: "Clothes make the man." We might adapt this familiar saying, making it a reminder to us of this Corporal Work of Mercy of clothing the naked by saying "clothes make the Christian."

Father, quicken my spirit to be able to slough off the excess material things of this world. May I go through life freed from the burdens of excess belongings. Sharpen my vision, so that I might be alert to my own "excess baggage" in life and be awake to those who are in need of my excess.

To shelter the homeless

In reflecting on the Corporal Works of Mercy, it becomes clear that while they are always in vogue, at times, one or the other of them rises to more prominence, either because of our own particular situation in life or because of the situation in our culture. For us at the present time, sheltering the homeless is a Work of Mercy that is in prominence in our milieu.

Jesus identified Himself with the homeless. In Luke's gospel, hear Jesus saying, "The foxes have lairs, the birds of the sky have nests, but the son of man has nowhere to lay his head" (Lk 9:58).

It's good for us to remember this, as sometimes we identify the homeless as "them" as opposed to "us." But, as much as the local literature on homelessness should have made clear to us, the step from "us" to homelessness can be a very short one. It can be a single missed pay-check, or a slight economic down-turn, a simple accident, a fire or a flood resulting in the in-capacity of the wage earner in a family, or . . . I think you get the point. Many of the homeless are people like you and me.

Our response? In our Columbus area, we are fortunate to have the Community Shelter Board which oversees and coordinates our re-sponse to the needs of the homeless. Support of the Community Shelter Board is certainly one way in which we put this Work of Mercy into action. Many communities offer similar op-portunities to shelter the homeless.

But this doesn't exhaust our possibilities or our responsibilities. Many of us have a more personal relationship with a shelter organiza-tion or group, such as the Interfaith Network which organizes families to feed and shelter a homeless family on a regular, but rotating basis. Some of us have relatives who, for one reason or another, are numbered among the homeless and look expectantly to us for shelter.

While our local homeless are a significant group, we know that when we raise our eyes from the local situation to the world view, the problem becomes a hundredfold more acute. These people, too, are our brothers and sisters.

Certainly we practice this Work of Mercy when we contribute to disaster relief collections or support organizations like Catholic Relief Services, which serve the basic material needs of people throughout the world. Even when we contribute to mission collections, we aid the homeless. A large part of our missionary dollars go to providing the basic human needs of the people with whom we seek to share the faith.

We describe this activity as pre-evangelization, which is a post-Vatican II term that makes a great deal of sense. After all, it's hard to tell a person that Jesus loves him or her, and that we are all brothers and sisters, when we live in a home and they live on the street. Pre-evangelization is a concrete sign of the Gospel message in action.

Even if we aren't linked with a shelter group, or are not the type to associate with a housing rights activist group, we are challenged to keep an open attitude towards the homeless and support the efforts of those who champion their causes, even if only in our heart of hearts.

As Catholics, we are especially challenged to be open to the homeless. Recall Jesus' description of the last judgment. One of the positive works He attributes to those on His right hand is, "I was a stranger and you welcomed me into your home" (Mt 25:35).

Let's make sure that for all of us the "welcome mat," which we find so often at our doors, is truly indicative of the message within.

And let's make sure that that same welcome mat is at the door of our hearts.

"Porta patet; cor magis."
"The door is open; the heart even more so."

Father, may my heart and my door be open to the homeless, and to all others who come to me in need. May I offer shelter to those who are homeless in the sure hope that You will offer the shelter of eternal life to me in the moment of judgment.

Visiting the sick is best done in person. Still, we can do it vicariously when a personal visit is impossible. A phone call, a card, flowers, or some other remembrance which brightens the day of a sick person carries the message of our personal care and concern.

Part of our visit should evidence our concern for the total welfare of the sick person. A corporeal "pick me up" can be blended with a spiritual lift. This can often contribute as much to one's physical healing, as does medicine or rest. So during our visit to the sick, we might pray together, or discuss the spiritual aspect of sickness and healing, or promise our continued prayers for restoration of health.

A practical note concerning the visitation of the sick, especially applicable in hospital situations, is contained in what was presented to me as the "Three B Rule" — be brief, be positive, be gone.

It requires strength and attention to receive a visitor; so be brief. Sickness brings out our own worries, concern, and sadness; so be positive. The purpose of a visit is to express our concern and our empathy. This can be done in a very short time; so be gone.

The practice of visiting the sick can easily be extended to a continued concern and compassion for them, extending even to those sick men and women whom we do not know personally.

Part of the mandate of our baptismal call is that we care for all the sick members of our community, not just those whom we know personally.

This concern and compassion can be expressed most simply and effectively through prayer. Perhaps just a little more attention is required on our part when in the General Intercessions we pray for the sick whether all together or by name. This same practice of praying attentively for the sick can be carried over in our daily prayer.

Father, help me to console the sick, as Your Son did during His time on earth. May my visitations, words, and actions evidence Your Spirit of compassion and bring peace, consolation, and healing to our sisters and brothers who are suffering.

when we periodically "touch base" with those left behind during this adjustment time. Helping them to cope with their own loss is a significant part of "burying the dead."

And for the Christian, all of this should be done with the attitude of Jesus. Jesus knew that Lazarus was going to rise again. There was no doubt of that in His mind. As we bury the dead, we too must stir up our conviction of the resurrection of the dead.

"Those who live in the Lord never see each other for the last time."

Father, through my prayers may I be of assistance to those who have died, helping them into Your Kingdom of peace and joy. Let me be a Simon of Cyrene to those who have lost a loved one. May I help them to carry their cross with Jesus and to accept Your will.

To visit the imprisoned

I have saved consideration of this Corporal Work of Mercy until last, as I believe it is one which our modern society offers the least opportunity for most of us to practice literally. In our complex society, many just do not have the opportunity of visiting the imprisoned.

Not that no opportunities exist. There are occasions when we might join parish groups which visit the imprisoned on a regular basis to bring the Eucharist, or to take part in a liturgy or para-liturgical service, or to bring some other religious benefit. At the Christmas season, there are groups which prepare and distribute small gift items to those who are imprisoned.

When we think about the imprisoned, it is important for us to keep in mind that these are people — men and women like ourselves. We

PART III

Spiritual Works of Mercy

ample of this is found in the story of Jesus and the woman at the well. Jesus is gentle, so gentle that, despite the correction, she runs to bring her friends to meet Him. Jesus is kind. He offers the woman a share in the "living waters" of faith. Jesus shows care and concern for the woman and her life situation. But still, He admonishes. As the woman herself so succinctly summarized it: "He told me everything I ever did!" (Jn 4:29).

And his first disciples certainly got this message. Reflect for instance on the last lines of the letter of St. James: "My brothers, the case may arise among you of someone straying from the truth, and of another bringing him back. Remember this, the person who brings a sinner back from his way will save his soul from death and cancel a multitude of sins" (Jm 5:19-20).

Parents, teachers and priests have a special responsibility here towards their children, their students, their communities. They must exercise authority in this arena of admonishment.

There are two commentaries about "admonishing the sinner" I would offer.

The first is summed up in a saying of Pope John XXIII about bishops. He said, "A bishop must see everything; remember much; but say very little." The lesson here is easily grasped and easily applied to the situations of life. We must know when our admonition will help and when it will be ignored or actually worsen the situation. This can be a difficult call. Here's where prayer and the direction of the Spirit is indispensable.

The second commentary: When we seek to admonish, we most often err by falling into the pattern of sternness or harshness, as if these could clarify the message. You know, "the louder I speak, the more you get the message." Most often these attributes generate much heat but little light. Consider rather the approach of Jesus with the woman at the well, the woman caught in adultery, the betrayal of Judas, the denial of Peter. Jesus admonished in all of these situations, but He did it with the utmost gentleness, with charity, and with compassion. Let us ask the Spirit to help us to be open to moments when we can admonish the sinner with gentleness and compassion.

Father, give me a gentle and wise heart when confronted with the sinner. May my gentleness draw that person close to You and may my wisdom open his or her heart to Your forgiving and healing love.

but not exclusively. Those who teach or who are placed over others, especially youth, do have a special responsibility. But I think everyone of us has the responsibility to teach. And remember, we not only teach by talking to people, we teach also by the way we live. The old adage proves true, "actions speak louder than words."

I learned this lesson from my own father. I never observed my father going to bed — at home, on vacation, anywhere — without first kneeling down beside the bed and saying his night prayer. That example taught me more about prayer and the place which prayer was to have in my life, than many of the sophisticated courses which I followed in theology or the heavy volumes which I read on prayer.

Instruct the ignorant — the spiritually ignorant are all around us. We are all spiritually ignorant to some degree. At the same time, we all have some spiritual knowledge, education or experience which we can share with others.

Because our culture does not prize this activity of "instructing the ignorant," few of us are sensitized to it. And innumerable opportunities to practice this Spiritual Work of Mercy pass by unnoticed. We might well begin to sharpen our practice of this work by praying for the grace to recognize and capitalize on these small opportunities of life to share spiritual knowledge with others.

Instructing the ignorant can be just a matter of attention to the way we live. The example which we give is a most effective, if silent, "teacher" of others. Our style of life, our language, our treatment of others, our readiness to forgive, our patience with the inconveniences and scrapes of life are powerful instructors to those around us.

President Bush likes to speak of the face of our nation being transformed through the individual and seemingly small activities of interested citizens, forming a "thousand points of light." Think how the spiritual climate could be improved by thousands of us using the little opportunities which come our way each day to "instruct the ignorant." We would surely form a "thousand points of spiritual light," so aptly described in the book of Daniel thousands of years ago: "Then the wise shall shine brightly like the splendor of the firmament, and those who lead the many to justice shall be like the stars forever" (Dn 12:3).

Father, bestow on me the gift of wisdom, to recognize and receive the "teaching" of others. May that same gift of wisdom enable me to identify my own grasp on Your truth. Finally, may I have the gift of courage, enabling me to share that truth with my sisters and brothers.

To counsel the doubtful

When we talk about counseling, most people in our society think about the work of experts in this field. In truth, the practice of this Spiritual Work of Mercy most often lies between the work of these experts and the comic strip situation pictured in Lucy sitting behind her great box stand with her shingle advertising "Psychiatric Advice — 5¢."

Don't think that you have to be an "expert" to give counsel to another. One of the bits of irony in our country is that people are willing to seek advice from total strangers — like Ann Landers or Dear Abby or horoscopes — rather than turn to their own sisters and brothers who are connected to them with special bonds of love, and who are privy to the situations in which they find themselves.

Giving counsel is not always as difficult as

one might imagine. Often if we just listen, if we just give another the opportunity to talk, that person will discover the solution to the problem in the very presentation of the difficulty. So offering counsel is often not anything more than respectful listening. And to listen is not beyond any of us!

Perhaps the question here then, is how approachable are we? How receptive are we to others, and to their problems and concerns? Do we take the time to listen to people? Again, note the irony in the fact that people in our society are ready to write and ask advice for their problems from people whom they do not even know. Perhaps this willingness indicates that there are not enough "listeners" among their family and friends.

Even when more than respectful listening is required, we need not despair. We all know from experience how helpful a word of encouragement or support has been. We know what help a suggestion given to us has been when we were in a state of doubt or lacked conviction as to the direction in which we might move.

There are times, however, when more direct counsel is called for. Consider the story of Jesus and the doubting Thomas. Jesus gave clear and direct counsel to Thomas: "Take your finger and examine my hand. Put your hand into my side. Do not persist in your unbelief, but believe" (Jn 20:27).

We should not hesitate to suggest a professional counselor when this is indicated. Again, a suggestion from a friend or from one who has shown genuine interest can often help a person in need of professional counseling to overcome the natural reluctance to seek this help.

More, recall Jesus' directions to the disciples who were out fishing, casting about after a night of fruitless effort (Jn 21:1-7).

These are moments in which we must rely on our own expertise, on our own experience in life, and, most fully of all, on the guidance of the Holy Spirit. With these aids, we "launch out in the deep" of counseling the doubtful.

Father, grant me, like Solomon, a "listening heart," an understanding heart, to judge and to distinguish right from wrong. May I listen with wisdom, discernment, strength, and tender affection. And, may I speak Your truth in loving simplicity.

To comfort the sorrowful

Again, we begin our consideration of this Spiritual Work of Mercy with a reflection of the example of Jesus. In the gospels, we find many examples of Jesus engaging in this Work of Mercy. Recall the stories of Jesus and the widow of Naim, the centurion with the sick child, Bartimaeus, the ten lepers, Lazarus' sisters, the women of Jerusalem, the women at the Resurrection scene. There is indeed a litany of examples in the life of Jesus of Him comforting the sorrowful.

We also find a litany of opportunities to practice this Work of Mercy in the life of each of us. We reach out to the emotional side of a fellow human being in extending this comfort; and these opportunities are manifold. In comforting the sorrowful, we give of ourself, and that giving assuages the grief of that person.

Consider what opportunities parents have to put this Work of Mercy into practice, as their children come to them and share the little sorrows of their lives with them.

But not just children suffer. "Life is difficult," as Scott Peck puts it so starkly in the opening line of his *The Road Less Traveled*. All of us must expect suffering to be a part of life.

For most of us, one of the chief ways in which we see people sorrowing is when they are confronted by the death of a loved one. With our belief in the Resurrection and our trust in the goodness of God, we stand in the ideal position to offer comfort to another at the time of a death. Do we respond? And do we respond with a spiritual message which is drawn out of our Catholic heritage? There are many, many other sufferings in life, as we all know from personal experience.

Another common suffering which we see others wrestling with is employment. They may be either looking for work, or struggling with a difficult job.

And who among us does not have sufferings within his or her own family or extended family? There are difficult situations or problems confronting every family. And once more, we have in our approach to family life and our paradigms for the role of father, mother, family member, the wherewithal from which to extend solid comfort to families in sorrow.

I think the obstacle to comforting the sorrowful stems from the fact that sorrow is so common. We all have our sorrows! The question becomes: Whose sorrows do we notice and address? Do we see and respond to the sufferings of others? Or, do we focus in on our own little world and our own sufferings?

Focusing on our own sorrows leads to a double frustration. First, we miss the opportunities to see and respond to the sufferings of others. Second, we most often lack the ability to comfort ourself in the midst of our own sorrows. And so, focusing in on the sorrow only increases our discomfort.

Conversely, looking out at the sufferings of others, both gives us opportunity to comfort them in their sorrows and, at the same time, helps to keep our own sorrows in proper perspective.

Father, as my own experiences in life have taught me to see the rainbow of Your love through the prism of my tears, so may I help others to that same vision. May my sorrow teach me to be sensitive, empathetic, and responsive to the sorrows of others.

To bear wrongs patiently

This is one of that special class of Works of Mercy about which I spoke earlier; entirely beyond the comprehension of our secular society.

Our society doesn't counsel the patient bearing of wrongs. It counsels the exact opposite. It encourages the prompt and aggressive pursuit of redress for every wrong — real or imagined.

The only reasonable explanation for the patient bearing of wrongs done to us is found in our belief that God Himself is the ultimate dispenser of justice, and that we acknowledge the presence of this just God within both ourself and others.

There is a natural inclination in the human person for justice. He or she wants to do justice to others, and wants justice done in return. This natural inclination stirs us to rise up in defense whenever we suffer a wrong. Our Christian realization that God Himself will, in the end, right every injustice softens this natural human reaction.

More, our patient bearing of wrongs brings benefit to our fellow human beings. Often it is our patient endurance that brings that other person to a realization of the wrong that he or she has done. At the least, our patient endurance often dissuades him or her from further injustice.

Life is filled with opportunities to "bear wrongs patiently." Almost every time we drive an automobile, we are presented with such opportunities. Another driver may move too slowly in front of us, or too swiftly behind us, or move over in front of us at an exit, or move towards a parking spot which we had already "scoped out." In all of these instances we can bear patiently the real or imagined wrong that is done us.

In business or civic meetings, we also are often confronted with opportunities to bear wrongs patiently. There is the situation where one who has collaborated with us on a project takes more of the credit than is his or her due, or incorrectly insinuates that some error or miscalculation is to be laid at our feet.

At home, how often family members misinterpret our words or actions, giving them a negative or critical slant which we never at all intended them to possess.

In all of these instances we "bear wrongs patiently." Again, there is a limit to this fore-bearance, most of the time quite clear and obvious. We cannot quietly allow another to lay a serious crime at our feet. Nor can we refrain from speaking out if our silence would scandalize or mislead others. In these instances, we have clearly reached and exceeded the bonds of "bearing wrongs patiently."

But these instances, as I have indicated, are usually quite obvious. And that is not the problem which faces us most often in today's society. The overwhelming majority of us find our difficulty in bearing the little wrongs of life patiently, for love of God and our brothers and sisters.

Father, when confronted with the "slings and arrows" of life launched at me by others, let me recall the sufferings which Your Son bore for me out of love. In the same spirit of love, enable me to bear wrongs patiently. Amen.

To forgive all injuries

This is another Spiritual Work of Mercy which simply does not compute in the culture in which we live. Our culture is peopled by individuals who are burdened-down with the baggage of unforgiven injuries. Neighborhoods, friendships, families, marriages, individual lives, are often torn apart by the pressures of these past injuries which continue to fester and build within us. Even though it would be to our advantage, we find it difficult to set aside past injuries.

The Christian motivation for setting aside these injuries, for practicing this Work of Mercy, parallels that outlined in our consideration of "bearing wrongs patiently," but with a new personal emphasis.

We forgive others because we see God reflected in their lives. We see the injuries which they have done us, as a reflection of their own human limitations, and not detractive of the goodness of God within them. Because we see and recognize this, we are ready to forgive.

We forgive others in accord with the teaching of Jesus. On innumerable occasions, in direct teaching and in parables, Jesus lifted up to us the virtue of forgiveness. He went so far as to say that the act of forgiveness makes us like His Father.

We forgive others in response to the example of Jesus. Who among us is not moved, when reading the story of the passion, by that prayer among those seven last words of Jesus in which He says, "Forgive them Father, for they know not what they do" (Lk 23:34)?

Finally, we forgive others because we know that this act brings us the forgiveness of our Father. Again, Jesus made this clear to us in His own teaching and in His own example.

We even make so bold as to pray in the prayer which Jesus Himself taught us: "Forgive us our trespasses, as we forgive those who trespass against us" (Mt 6:12). We pray for a forgiveness being extended to us which mirrors the forgiveness which we have extended to others.

This is the "personal emphasis" which I mentioned earlier. As Christians, we are motivated to forgive injuries by the realization that this is precisely the forgiveness for which we pray. More, it is exactly the forgiveness which we expect in response to our prayer to the Father. In effect, we ask Him to treat us at the end of our life exactly as we have treated others during the course of our lifetime.

Father, may the words "I forgive" live in my heart and come easily to my lips. May I be able to "forgive and forget" injuries done to me along the path of life. May forgiveness be a hallmark of my passage through life. And may that same forgiveness be a hallmark of my passage from this life.

To pray for the living and the dead

This final Spiritual Work of Mercy flows from our doctrine of "the communion of saints." We believe that there is an interrelationship which exists among us, a connection which survives even death. The "communion of saints" emphasizes that these bonds perdure from the living, to the souls in purgatory, to the saints in heaven. We are all one family.

Because we accept that we, the living, are all sisters and brothers in Christ, that we depend on one another, and that what happens to one does indeed affect the welfare of all, we pray for one another. In our prayer, we recognize the reality that what happens to one, affects all.

The words "pray for me" or "I will pray for you," then, are more than mere formalities, more than set expressions of our well-wishes for one another. They are a recognition of those bonds of community which exist among us. They are a commitment to a response to these ties of interdependency.

Our prayer for the living begins with those whom we love in a special way. That prayer extends out to those whom divine providence brings into our life through circumstances of work or leisure time. That prayer encompasses all who share commonalities of citizenship, religion, heritage, or culture. That prayer even extends to those least known and those least understood by us. That prayer literally encompasses all of the living.

But not even death breaks that chain of prayer. One of the consolations of life, especially in those dark or difficult moments of life, is that we are supported by the prayers of the saints in heaven. Again, that doctrine of the communion of saints ensures us that those who have reached heaven continue to care about all of us, and, in a special way, about those bound to them by some of those commonalities which I mentioned earlier, as well as those who implore their help through prayer.

This doctrine of the communion of saints, brings us tremendous comfort when death comes to a loved one or friend. This teaching assures us that death is not the end. We are separated, but the separation is not forever. Even more, this doctrine tells us that we are not helpless in the face of death. Those bonds mentioned earlier continue. Our prayers can assist the souls of our beloved departed on the way to heaven.

As in the case of all of these Spiritual Works of Mercy, though directed outwards towards others, the benefits also redound to self.

By our prayers for others, we become aware of our relationship and our interdependence. We become more aware of the fact that we are "stewards" of creation and created things, and not their permanent owners.

Our prayers for the dead relieve our own feelings of frustration and helplessness. These same prayers help prepare us for our own turn at that doorway through which there is no returning. We pass through fortified by the realization that others will, as we have through the course of our lifetime, remember us and support us on the journey to heaven, our final home.

Father, may I become more and more conscious that, in calling You my "Father," I make myself brother or sister to all of Your creation. May I express that solidarity with my sisters and brothers by praying for them, presenting the needs and the intentions of the living, recalling the good deeds of the dead. May my loving concern for them be yet another sign that I am indeed Your child, child of an all-loving Father.

Conclusion

Throughout the second and third parts of these reflections, we have discussed the meaning and the application of the Corporal and Spiritual Works of Mercy. Perhaps we might conclude our reflection on the practical applications of "the law of love" by considering our own motives for practicing them.

In the pragmatic sense, these works appear to be noble and worthwhile endeavors. Many of them respond to yearnings and noble aspirations that are part of our human nature. But that is not the explanation of our practice of these works.

We turn to the Bible to find the true reason for practicing these Works of Mercy. As we have repeatedly seen the Works of Mercy illustrated and lived out in the life of Jesus, it is in the gospels that we find a clear and fitting explanation of our pursuit of these Works of Mercy.

Let us look at the gospel of Matthew. The scene is the final judgment. The sheep will be separated from the goats. To the sheep, to those on His right hand, the King will say, "Come you have my Father's blessing! Inherit the kingdom prepared for you from the creation of the world. For I was hungry and you gave me food; I was thirsty and you gave me drink; I was a stranger, you welcomed me; naked and you clothed me; I was ill and you comforted me; in prison and you came to visit me" (Mt 25:34-36).

In response to their surprised question "when," the King answers: "I assure you, as often as you did it for one of my least brothers, you did it for me" (Mt 25:40).

The lesson is sharp and clear. Jesus lives within each of our brothers and sisters. In responding to their needs, we respond to His needs. We perform these Corporal and Spiritual Works of Mercy, then, because we recognize Jesus' presence in our sisters and brothers. In responding to the needs of our brothers and sisters, we respond to Jesus Himself.

Look at the people in your own life. Try to see them in a new light. Try to see them against the background of this last judgment scene. Try to see Jesus dwelling in each of them.

It is usually easier to see Jesus in those whom we love. It becomes more difficult to recognize Him and His presence in those towards whom we are indifferent. It is a heart-rending struggle to see and recognize Jesus, even in those whom we do not like. Still, Jesus lives in all of them, and He will reward us in direct proportion to our having recognized and served Him in all our brothers and sisters. This is the only description of the last judgment He gives us. And this is the only criterion that He reveals to us on which our future life depends.

"I assure you, as often as you did it for one of my least brothers, you did it for me." As we reflect on these Works of Mercy, as we attempt to integrate them into our own lives, let us never lose sight of the basic reason why we practice them.

We perform them, not for notice or praise, not to be well thought of or respected, not to "feel good" or find fulfillment of our natural inclinations. No, as Christians we strive to practice these Works of Mercy because Jesus lives in each human being. And in servicing their needs, we serve Jesus Himself.

1